4

Ingredients

Christmas

Baby Bowl

*Home-Cooked Meals for Happy, Healthy Babies
and Toddlers*

4 Ingredients

*More than 400 Quick, Easy, and Delicious Recipes
Using 4 or Fewer Ingredients*

4 Ingredients Gluten-Free

*More than 400 New and Exciting Gluten-Free Recipes
Using 4 or Fewer Ingredients*

4
Ingredients

Christmas

Recipes for a Simply Yummy Holiday

Kim McCosker

ATRIA PAPERBACK

New York   London   Toronto   Sydney   New Delhi

ATRIA PAPERBACK

A Division of Simon & Schuster, Inc.
1230 Avenue of the Americas
New York, NY 10020

First Atria Paperback edition October 2012

ATRIA PAPERBACK and colophon are trademarks of Simon & Schuster, Inc.

For information about special discounts for bulk purchases,
please contact Simon & Schuster Special Sales at
1-866-506-1949 or business@simonandschuster.com.

The Simon & Schuster Speakers Bureau can bring authors
to your live event. For more information or to book an event,
contact the Simon & Schuster Speakers Bureau at
1-866-248-3049 or visit our website at www.simonspeakers.com.

Manufactured in the United States of America

10 9 8 7 6 5 4 3 2 1

Library of Congress Cataloging-in-Publication Data is available.

ISBN: 978-1-4516-7801-7
ISBN: 978-1-4516-7802-4 (ebook)

Contents

Introduction

I love Christmas and everything about it. Festive fare, family and friends, and a little time out from the business of life. Yet as we all know, it can also be an overwhelming amount of work! Clever entertaining to me is creating the illusion that I have been slaving away diligently in the kitchen, meticulously planning the menu, setting the table, choosing a theme, color, flowers, and prepping as much as I can so that when the time arrives, I too can actually enjoy myself.

As with all of my books in the 4 Ingredients series, *4 Ingredients Christmas* is all about making cooking and entertaining at home fast and fabulous. I truly believe that as long as you have fresh ingredients, four are really all you need to come up with something delicious and impressive. (Special note: Salt, pepper, and water are not included in the four ingredients.) In this book, you'll find recipes perfect for Christmas Eve treats, holiday brunches, and formal family dinners. Your table will be full of amazing-looking dishes that will appear much more complicated, time-consuming, and expensive than they actually are.

Where I live in Caloundra, along Australia's gorgeous Sunshine Coast, December 25 is in the middle of our summer. Christmas to me means outdoor parties, grilled fish, fresh cherries and watermelon, ice cream, and ice-cold cocktails. It means decorating with pink petunias and bright orange nasturtiums in addition to a festive Christmas tree and hints of red and green throughout the house. The holiday wouldn't feel complete without traditional dishes like Citrus-Glazed Ham, Maple & Pepper–Glazed Turkey, Seasoned Roast Vegetables, Plum Pudding, and Christmas cake (your fruitcake), which is why I've included glorious recipes for those in this book. But I also wanted American cooks to consider a Southern Hemisphere twist to the holiday with Watermelon & Feta Bites (you can replace the watermelon with pears, dates, or whatever lovely fruit is in season where you are), Ruby Jeweled Lobster Salad, and Caramel Ice Cream. Many of the desserts and sweet treats you'll find here don't require baking. For me, it's a way of keeping my kitchen calm and cool for the many friends and family passing through it. For those of you at home in a winter wonderland, these dishes will help save time and oven space. By way of the beautiful photographs taken by Megan Slade, *4 Ingredients Christmas* represents what my table looks like on Christmas Day and the day after . . . and the day after that . . .

The fact is, *4 Ingredients Christmas* isn't just a Christmas cookbook. My husband requests the Wild Mushroom Beef Wellington every year for his February birthday. My dad's July birthday wouldn't be the same without his beloved Chicken & Port Pâté. My sister-in-law, Nelly, asks for the Heavenly Halloumi Skewers every time she visits (which is a lot—*"Hi, Nelly!"*). Sunday dinner is so much better with Roast Pork & Crispy Crackling, and the Lime & Macadamia Fudge makes a simple, elegant thank-you gift any day of the year.

It is my hope that *4 Ingredients Christmas* will become your go-to cookbook for any occasion, be it Christmas, Thanksgiving, Mother's Day, birthdays, anniversaries, or special dinner parties with family and friends.

Stress no more, my lovelies!
Take a deep breath, pour a glass of wine,
and start to plan your menu from the simply yummy recipes within.

Happy entertaining!

Kim x

The Night Before Christmas

MAGIC REINDEER DUST

MAKES 1 SPRINKLE BAG

¼ cup oatmeal (rolled oats)
2 tablespoons sugar
1 tablespoon edible glitter

In a small plastic sandwich bag or cellophane gift bag, mix all the ingredients together. Tie with a ribbon. On Christmas Eve, give to your children to . . .

*Sprinkle on the lawn
at night,*

*The moon will make
it sparkle bright.*

*As Santa's reindeer
fly and roam,*

*This will guide them
to your home.*

REINDEER'S FAVORITE DIP

**SERVES 8 REINDEER
(OR PEOPLE)**

5 carrots, peeled and cut into 1-inch pieces
1½ packages Boursin cheese (5.2 ounces each) or one 8-ounce tub cream cheese with chives
2 tablespoons tahini (sesame paste)
1 tablespoon finely chopped fresh chives

Cook the carrots in a saucepan of boiling water for 10 minutes, or until just tender. Drain and set aside for 10 minutes to cool. Place the carrots, cheese, and tahini in a food processor and process until smooth. Season with sea salt and pepper. Transfer to a serving bowl. Cover with plastic wrap and place in the fridge until ready to serve. Sprinkle with the chives just before serving.

REINDEER TREATS

MAKES 16 WAFERS

8 ounces Cheddar or Monterey Jack cheese, grated (2 cups)
8 tablespoons (1 stick) butter, sliced
1 cup all-purpose flour
Pinch of cayenne pepper

Using a mixer with a paddle or a wooden spoon, mix all the ingredients until well blended. Shape into a roll about 1 inch in diameter. Wrap in parchment paper and freeze for 30 minutes, or until firm enough to cut. Preheat the oven to 350°F. Cut the roll into ½-inch slices, place on an ungreased baking sheet, and bake for 15 to 18 minutes, or until light golden brown. Serve warm or at room temperature.

Sprinkle on the lawn at night
The moon will make it sparkle bright
As Santa's reindeer fly and roam
This will guide them to your home.

Brunch

Almond Bread

MAKES 30 SLICES

4 egg whites
½ cup sugar
1 cup all-purpose flour
5 ounces whole almonds

Preheat the oven to 350°F and line a 9-inch loaf pan with parchment paper. Using an electric mixer, beat the egg whites until stiff. Gradually add the sugar and beat for 4 minutes, or until meringue consistency. Fold in the flour and almonds. Spoon the batter into the loaf pan and bake for 45 minutes. Remove from the oven and lower the oven temperature to 260°F. Allow the loaf to cool completely in the pan, then turn out of the pan onto a cutting board and peel off the parchment paper. Using a really sharp knife, cut into 30 slices. Place the slices on a baking sheet and return to the oven for 10 minutes, or until golden and crisp.

Bacon & Avocado Bruschetta

Crisp bacon and creamy avocado are complemented beautifully
with a twist of lemon in this delightful Christmas brunch dish.

SERVES 4

6 slices bacon, cut crosswise in half
12 slices crusty French or Italian bread, ¼ inch thick, cut on the diagonal
1 Hass avocado, split and pitted
Slivered peel and juice of ½ lemon

Preheat the broiler. In a skillet, cook the bacon until nice and crisp.
Drain on paper towels. Place the bread on a broiling pan and broil
until lightly toasted on one side. Flip the slices and toast on the other
side. Scoop the avocado into a bowl, add lemon juice to taste, mash
well, and season with salt and pepper. Spread a good tablespoon
of avocado onto each toast. Top with a piece of bacon, a few drops
of lemon juice, a little lemon peel, and a twist of cracked pepper.

Breakfast Trifles

Inspired by the classic layered dessert, this is a colorful, healthy way to start the day, and it's super quick to whip up.

SERVES 8

4 cups muesli or granola
12 strawberries, washed, hulled, and quartered
½ fresh pineapple, peeled, cored, and chopped
2 cups plain Greek-style yogurt

In eight 8-ounce glasses, layer a couple of tablespoons each of muesli, then fruit, then yogurt. Repeat until full, ending with a dollop of yogurt.

Optional: Substitute chopped clementine segments for the pineapple.

Chocolate-Filled Crepes

I cannot count the number of times I have made this recipe
in the last decade. This is my boys' favorite brunch dish.

SERVES 8

2 eggs

1 cup milk

2¼ cups all-purpose flour

Nutella, for filling

In a large bowl, lightly whisk together the eggs, milk, and flour with
1 cup water (the batter will be quite thin). Heat a nonstick skillet
(brush with a little melted butter, if needed). Pour a quarter cup
of batter into the pan and swirl in a circular motion outward so
the batter spreads evenly. Cook for 2 minutes, or until the bottom
is light brown. Flip to cook the other side for another minute.
Remove and spread with Nutella. Seal by folding the crepe in
thirds, or roll and cut in half. Repeat until all the batter is gone.

Croque Monsieur

Such a simple idea and a family favorite.

SERVES 8

16 slices sourdough bread
¼ cup Dijonnaise or 2 tablespoons Dijon mustard
mixed with 2 tablespoons mayonnaise
8 ounces sliced ham
8 ounces Gruyère cheese, grated (2 cups)

Preheat a sandwich press. Spread 8 slices of the bread with the Dijonnaise. Top with ham and cheese and season with salt and pepper. Place on the sandwich press (it's okay to work in batches if you can cook only a few at a time). Top each with another slice of bread, close the press, and cook for 2 to 3 minutes, until the bread is golden brown and the cheese has melted.

Tip: A Croque Monsieur becomes a "Madame" when a fried egg is placed on top because of its resemblance to a woman's bosom! And if you don't have a sandwich press, just butter the outside of the sandwiches and cook in a medium-hot nonstick skillet for 2 to 3 minutes per side, flipping once.

Eggs with Smoked Salmon Fingers

SERVES 8

8 eggs
6 slices dense sandwich bread, crusts trimmed
1 tablespoon butter, softened
10 ounces smoked salmon, cut into long 1-inch-wide strips

Place the eggs in a saucepan, cover with cold water by about
1 inch, and bring to a boil. Cover the pan, remove from the heat,
and let sit for 6 minutes. Drain and set aside for 10 minutes.
Preheat the broiler to high. Cut the bread into long strips and
arrange on a broiling pan. Broil for 1 to 2 minutes on each side,
until toasted. Spread the toasts with the butter. Wrap the strips
of salmon around the toasts. Place the eggs in egg cups and
carefully slice off the tops. Serve with the "salmon fingers" to dip.

Optional: Substitute thin slices of ham or prosciutto for the salmon.

Grilled Fruit & Ricotta Stacks

This stunning brunch never ceases to impress!

MAKES 4 STACKS

2 pears, cut into long slices
2 bananas, sliced on the diagonal
4 tablespoons fresh ricotta
2 tablespoons honey

Heat the broiler or a grill pan to high. Cook the pear slices for 3 minutes, flipping once, until lightly browned. Layer the pear and banana slices on four plates. Top each with a dollop of ricotta and drizzle with honey.

Optional: This is also delicious using apple instead of pear, or a combination of both.

Ham & Egg Quiches

Gluten-free and glorious!

MAKES 8 QUICHES

8 ultrathin round slices ham

8 eggs

4 ounces Cheddar cheese, grated (1 cup)

2 tablespoons chopped fresh parsley

Preheat the oven to 350°F. Line 8 muffin pan cups or custard cups with the ham. Whisk the eggs well and season with sea salt and cracked pepper. Divide the eggs evenly among the cups. Sprinkle each with cheese and parsley. Bake for 20 minutes, or until golden and set.

Pancakes with Caramelized Banana

Once I was pouring the caramel sauce onto my six-year-old's pancakes when he said, "Mummy, it's like a river of toffee!" How true his words were.

SERVES 8

4 tablespoons (½ stick) butter
¾ cup light brown sugar
4 bananas, thickly sliced on the diagonal
16 pancakes (homemade or store-bought)

Put the butter and sugar in a nonstick skillet. Over medium heat, stir to melt the butter and dissolve the sugar. Add the bananas, reduce the heat, and cook for 3 minutes, stirring occasionally, until the bananas are coated with caramel. Heat the pancakes in the microwave for 30 seconds, stack on serving plates, and top with the divinely caramelized bananas.

Optional: To whip up your own pancakes, beat 1 egg, 1 cup milk, and 1 cup self-rising flour with ½ teaspoon grated nutmeg. Heat an 8-inch nonstick skillet over low to medium heat. Dollop in large spoonfuls of batter and cook until the bubbles burst on the surface and the edges start to go dry. Flip and cook the other side until golden.

Nibbles

Asparagus Wraps

This appetizer is both impressive and easy to
make, and the plate is always left clean.

MAKES 16 SPEARS

8 slices prosciutto
1 bunch asparagus (16 spears), woody ends snapped off
1 tablespoon extra virgin olive oil
1 tablespoon balsamic vinegar

Preheat the oven to 350°F. Use a sharp knife to cut each prosciutto
slice lengthwise into two long strips. Wrap a piece of prosciutto around
each asparagus spear, creating a spiral effect. Place the wrapped
spears on a baking sheet, drizzle lightly with the oil and vinegar,
and season with sea salt and pepper. Bake for 5 minutes. Flip the
spears over and bake for another 5 minutes, or until the asparagus
is just tender. Transfer to a serving plate and serve immediately.

Baked Brie with Macadamia Praline

This is a perennial. It blossoms in all seasons!

SERVES 8

¼ cup light brown sugar
¼ cup chopped macadamia nuts
2 tablespoons brandy
One 7-ounce wheel Brie cheese

In a small bowl, stir together the sugar, nuts, and brandy. Cover and chill for at least 2 hours. Preheat the oven to 400°F. Place the Brie on an ovenproof platter and bake for 4 minutes, or until slightly softened. Spread the praline mixture in an even layer on top of the Brie and bake for 3 minutes more, or until the sugar melts. This will become an entertaining regular!

Optional: Serve with wedges of freshly sliced apple and pear.

Cheese Board

SERVES 8

8 ounces Brie cheese
8 ounces Cheddar cheese (your choice of sharpness), plain or peppered
16 dates
8 ounces red grapes

A cheese board is a welcome indulgence at most gatherings.
I will usually complement a soft cheese with a hard cheese.
As a rough guideline, allow a minimum of 2 ounces of cheese
per person when serving cheese at the start of a meal, and
3 ounces at the end. Provide a variety of crackers or fresh slices
of crusty bread as accompaniments with fresh, seasonal fruit
(grapes are listed here but can be easily replaced with pear or
apple) to refresh the palate and complement the cheese.

*Hint: Never serve cheese straight from the fridge. Cold temperatures
can make even the tastiest, ripest (and most expensive) cheeses taste
bland. Make sure the cheese has at least one hour to reach room
temperature before it is served in order to fully appreciate both its aroma
and flavor. And as my dad would say, "Don't forget the port!"*

Cucumber Ribbons & Shrimp

Go to page 51 to see how lovely Cucumber Ribbons & Shrimp look on a Tasting Plate.

SERVES 6

18 cooked large shrimp
1 large seedless cucumber
2 tablespoons Thai sweet chili sauce

Peel and devein the shrimp, leaving the tail intact, and rinse under cold running water. Trim the ends from the cucumber and, using a vegetable peeler, peel long, thin ribbons. Discard the seedy center core. Pleat a ribbon three or four times to form a ruffle, then on a toothpick, skewer 1 or 2 ribbons and 1 shrimp. Skewer each and drizzle gently with sweet chili sauce. Serve immediately on its own, or on the Tasting Plate on page 50.

Decadent Salmon Stacks

SERVES 8

6 slices bakery pumpernickel bread, crusts removed
One 8-ounce package light cream cheese, softened
4 ounces smoked salmon, finely chopped
4 ounces caviar or salmon roe

Line an 8- or 9-inch loaf pan with plastic wrap. Trim the bread so the slices fit in the pan in pairs in a snug layer. Stir together the cream cheese and salmon until soft and well blended; season with sea salt and pepper. Spread the cream cheese mixture on the bread. Flip over enough slices to line the bottom and place them in the pan, cream cheese side down. Continue the process until all the bread is used. Cover with plastic wrap and refrigerate for 2 to 3 hours, until firm. To serve, turn the loaf out of the pan onto a cutting board and carefully remove the plastic. Using a sharp knife, cut in half the long way and then crosswise to make eight pieces. Garnish each piece with a dollop of caviar. Serve immediately.

Optional: I had some fresh dill in my refrigerator, so I chopped a little of it into the cream cheese and salmon mixture for some added flavor, then used the remainder for garnish.

Oyster Trio

SERVES 8 TO 10

3 dozen raw oysters, freshly shucked, on the half shell

BACON, BALSAMIC & LEMON DRESSING

2 slices bacon, cut into ¼-inch squares

2 tablespoons balsamic vinegar

Finely shredded zest of ½ lemon

In a small saucepan over low to medium heat, cook the bacon, stirring occasionally, until crisp. Stir in the balsamic vinegar and lemon zest and season with salt and pepper. Allow to cool before spooning onto 12 of the oysters.

GINGER-WASABI MAYO

1 tablespoon freshly grated ginger

⅓ cup mayonnaise

1 teaspoon wasabi paste

1 tablespoon finely chopped pickled ginger

Stir together the grated ginger, mayonnaise, and wasabi until smooth. Spoon over 12 oysters and sprinkle with the pickled ginger.

OYSTERS MEXICANO

Finely shredded zest and juice of ½ lime

¼ cup guacamole, or mashed avocado seasoned with salt and pepper

12 corn chips or tortilla chips

Drizzle the lime juice over 12 oysters. Spoon on the guacamole, sprinkle with a little zest, and stud with a chip to serve.

Ricotta & Prosciutto Pies

MAKES 12 PIES

5 slices prosciutto
14 ounces fresh ricotta cheese
Leaves from 6 sprigs fresh thyme
1 bunch chives, chopped

Preheat the oven to 350°F. Cut the prosciutto into pieces and use it to line 12 mini muffin pan cups. Stir together the ricotta, thyme, and chives, and season with sea salt and cracked pepper. Distribute the cheese evenly among the cups. Bake for 15 minutes, or until set. Cool in the pan for 15 minutes before serving.

Optional: Top each with a cherry tomato half, cut side down, before baking.

Salmon Ceviche

SERVES 8

10 ounces skinless center-cut salmon fillet
1 lemon, peeled and cut in half lengthwise
1 red onion, thinly sliced into rings
2 tablespoons capers, drained

Place the salmon in the freezer for 10 minutes to firm up. Slice the salmon thinly and arrange on a serving plate, overlapping the slices slightly. Cut one half of the lemon into segments, removing all membrane. Scatter the onion, capers, and lemon segments over the salmon. Season with sea salt and cracked pepper and drizzle with the juice squeezed from the other lemon half. Cover, refrigerate, and marinate for 15 minutes.

Shrimp with a Trio of Dipping Sauces

SERVES 6

1 pound cooked, peeled shrimp (leave the tails on)

LEMONY AÏOLI

½ cup mayonnaise

1 clove garlic, crushed

2 tablespoons lemon juice

½ teaspoon grated lemon zest

MANGO SALSA

1 medium mango, peeled, pitted, and cubed (1 cup)

Grated zest and juice of ½ lime

1 tablespoon Thai sweet chili sauce

3 sprigs fresh cilantro, finely chopped

SWEET SOY SAUCE

2 tablespoons soy sauce

2 tablespoons honey

2 tablespoons oyster sauce

Arrange the shrimp on a serving platter. Stir or whisk together the ingredients for each sauce in a small bowl and season with sea salt and cracked pepper. Serve alongside the shrimp.

Skewer Duo

CHICKEN & CHORIZO SKEWERS

MAKES 8 SKEWERS

1 skinless, boneless chicken breast,
cut into 24 (1-inch) cubes

1 link fully cooked chorizo sausage,
cut into 24 thin slices

Olive oil spray

½ cup salsa

If using bamboo skewers, soak for at least
30 minutes. Heat a grill, grill pan, or cast-iron
skillet to medium. Onto each skewer, thread a
piece of chicken and a slice of chorizo; repeat
twice per skewer. Spray lightly with oil, then
grill for 4 minutes on each side, or until cooked
through, flipping a couple of times to evenly
cook. Serve warm with salsa as a dipping sauce.

HEAVENLY HALLOUMI SKEWERS

MAKES 8 SKEWERS

24 large basil leaves

6 ounces halloumi cheese, cut into 24 cubes

8 oil-packed sun-dried tomatoes,
drained and cut in thirds

3 tablespoons balsamic glaze (see Tip
on page 50 to make your own)

If using bamboo skewers, soak for at least
30 minutes. Heat a grill, grill pan, or cast-iron
skillet to medium. Onto each skewer, thread
a basil leaf, a cube of halloumi, and a piece
of tomato; repeat twice. Grill the skewers
for 2 minutes on each side, or until golden,
flipping once. Season with salt and pepper
and drizzle with balsamic glaze. Serve warm.

Sweet Fig & Gorgonzola Pizza

This is simply stunning on a holiday table.

SERVES 8

4 flatbreads, such as pocketless pita or naan
8 ounces Gorgonzola cheese, crumbled (2 cups)
6 fresh figs, stemmed and cut into quarters or eighths (depending on size)
¼ cup honey

Preheat the oven to 350°F and line one or two baking sheets with parchment paper (depending on the size of the breads). Place the flatbreads on the baking sheet and sprinkle each with ½ cup Gorgonzola. Arrange the figs on top, then drizzle with honey and season with sea salt and pepper. Bake for 15 minutes, or until golden. Once out of the oven, slice and serve immediately.

Optional: Substitute an 8-ounce piece of Cambozola or Brie, rind and all, for the Gorgonzola in this recipe.

Tip: Fresh figs contain up to 80 percent water, with the highest levels of natural sugars. They are a brilliant source of energy and, like blueberries, are a great stimulant for the brain.

Tasting Plate

If you like, add Cucumber Ribbons & Shrimp
(page 34) to this tasty plate.

CHICKEN & PORT PÂTÉ

SERVES 8

4 tablespoons (½ stick) butter, softened
10 to 11 ounces chicken livers, trimmed
2 scallions (green onions), finely chopped
2 tablespoons port wine

Melt 2 tablespoons of the butter in a large
skillet. Cook the livers, in batches if necessary,
until just browned. Add the scallions and cook,
stirring, until the scallions are tender. Add the
port. Cook, uncovered, until almost all of the
liquid has evaporated. Transfer to a blender
or food processor and blend until smooth.
Add the remaining butter and blend until fully
incorporated and smooth. Transfer to a bowl and
refrigerate for at least 2 hours before serving.

*Hint: This recipe represents my first foray into the
world of homemade pâté, and it was extremely
successful. This is the perfect pâté, delicious on your
favorite crackers or small slices of toasted bread.*

WATERMELON & FETA BITES

MAKES 24 BITES

½ small seedless watermelon, rind removed
7 ounces feta cheese, cut into 24 cubes
24 mint leaves
2 tablespoons balsamic glaze (see Tip below)

Cut the watermelon into 24 (1-inch) cubes
and place on a serving platter. Top each with a
cube of feta and a mint leaf. Lightly drizzle with
balsamic glaze and spear each with a toothpick.

*Optional: Now, I know trying to find watermelon
in the United States around Christmas might be
as likely as winning the lottery, so try these instead:
figs, feta, and honey; pears and feta; or pitted dates
stuffed with feta and wrapped with prosciutto.*

*Tip: If you don't have balsamic glaze, simply make your
own: Pour ½ cup balsamic vinegar into a small skillet
and add 2 tablespoons light or dark brown sugar.
Cook over medium heat until syrupy. Set aside to cool.*

Soups & Salads

Arugula & Roquefort Soup

Adding blue cheese to almost anything will make the ordinary come alive. This soup is no exception. It's sensational!

SERVES 6 TO 8

6 cups vegetable stock
10 to 11 ounces arugula (about 6 cups)
8 ounces Roquefort or other blue cheese, crumbled (2 cups)
1¼ cups heavy cream

Bring the stock almost to a boil in a large saucepan. Add the arugula and gently simmer for 4 minutes, or until tender. Stir in the cheese and simmer for 1 minute, or until it starts to melt. Puree the soup in a blender, in batches if necessary, until smooth. Stir in the cream and season with cracked pepper. Reheat before serving and ladle into warmed bowls.

Carrot & Cilantro Soup

I fell in love with this flavorsome, healthy soup while
visiting friends in England. I hope you like it, too.

SERVES 8

2 quarts vegetable stock
2 onions, peeled and chopped
1 large bunch fresh cilantro, chopped (leaves and stems)
12 carrots, peeled and coarsely chopped

In a large saucepan, combine the stock, onions, cilantro, and carrots.
Bring to a boil, reduce the heat, and simmer for 20 minutes, or until the
carrots are tender. Season with sea salt and pepper. Puree the soup in
a blender, in batches if necessary, until smooth. Reheat before serving.
Ladle into warmed bowls and serve garnished with fresh cilantro leaves.

Crispy Salmon Salad

This is a fabulous lunch when you are entertaining—any time of year.

SERVES 8

12 ounces marinated feta cheese
3¼ pounds skinless salmon fillet, cubed
8 ounces fresh green beans, trimmed and blanched
1 bunch fresh dill, chopped

Drain the feta, saving the oil. Crumble the feta. Heat the oil in a large skillet until very hot. Add the salmon cubes and sear on all sides until crispy but still pink in the center (or cooked to your liking). In a large bowl, combine the green beans, feta, and dill and toss; add the salmon and gently fold in, taking care not to break the salmon cubes.

Optional: This is also delicious drizzled with a little fresh lemon juice.

Tip: If you can't find marinated feta, cut regular feta into small cubes and use 1 to 2 tablespoons olive oil to sear the salmon.

Entertainer's Timbale

While presenting on a cruise ship in November 2011, I asked a lady from the audience, who said she never entertained, to come up on stage with me and make this in front of six hundred people. She was so nervous—shaking, in fact! But in less than two minutes she had created exactly what you see here. She received a thunderous ovation!

SERVES 8

1¼ pounds thinly sliced smoked chicken
8 ounces seedless red grapes, quartered
3 ripe avocados, pitted, peeled, and thinly sliced
⅔ cup toasted pine nuts

To make individual timbales, stack the chicken, grapes, and avocado in eight 3-inch-diameter ring molds, repeating layers until all the ingredients are used. Gently press the contents down, turn over onto a serving plate, and carefully remove the rings. Sprinkle with the pine nuts and serve. This dish can also be made as one large salad. Simply place all the ingredients in a serving bowl, season, and toss together.

Optional: Drizzle with your favorite flavored oil or a squeeze of lemon juice.

Hint: A timbale is usually a dish of meat, fish, vegetables, or pasta molded into a cylinder tapered at one end. The ring molds for this dish can be bought at any kitchenware shop and are really easy to use.

Garden Salad

SERVES 8

2 bunches asparagus, woody ends snapped off
4 slices bacon, cut in half crosswise
7 ounces mixed baby lettuces or mesclun
¼ cup balsamic glaze (see Tip on page 50 to make your own)

Make an ice bath in a large bowl with cold water and plenty of ice cubes. In a large saucepan, bring 3 cups water to a boil. Add the asparagus and cook for 3 minutes, until bright green and crisp-tender. Using tongs, transfer the asparagus to the ice bath to stop cooking. Drain the asparagus when cool. Heat a nonstick skillet and cook the bacon for 4 to 5 minutes, until nice and crisp. Put the leaves on a large serving plate. Add the asparagus and bacon, season with sea salt and cracked black pepper, and toss lightly. Drizzle with the balsamic glaze and serve.

Optional: For a festive effect, sprinkle with bright, vibrant nasturtiums just before serving.

Mango, Avocado & Shrimp Salad

This is the quintessential Queensland salad: vibrant and tasty!

SERVES 4

2 large mangos
2 avocados
12 cooked shrimp, peeled and deveined
4 thin slices lime

Peel, pit, and slice the mangos and avocados. In individual glasses, layer the mango, avocado, and shrimp, ending with a lovely fresh shrimp (tail on or off). Drizzle the mango juice from the cutting board over each and season with salt and pepper. Chill, and when ready to serve, garnish with a slice of lime.

Optional: A variation is to use crispy bacon as a substitute for shrimp. This is a stunning salad served in a large glass bowl, lightly seasoned and tossed. Remember it for your next Fourth of July barbecue!

Ruby Jeweled Lobster Salad

SERVES 8

1 large bulb fennel, trimmed, stalks and fronds discarded
2 pomegranates
8 cooked rock lobster tails, shelled and deveined
4 oranges, peeled and segmented

Thinly slice or shave the fennel, discarding the hard core. Collect the ruby seeds from the pomegranates by chopping them open and scooping them out. Combine the seeds in a large bowl with the lobster and orange segments. Squeeze any remaining juice from your oranges over the salad. Toss gently, season with salt and pepper, and serve.

Optional: Use 2½ pounds cooked and peeled super colossal (U/12) shrimp as a substitute for the lobster.

Mains

Apple, Camembert & Potato Terrine

SERVES 6 AS A MAIN, 8 AS A SIDE

5 large boiling potatoes
6 tablespoons (¾ stick) butter
3 green apples, cored
10½ ounces Camembert cheese, chilled and very thinly sliced

In a large pot of lightly salted boiling water, boil the potatoes for
15 minutes (they won't be cooked through). Drain, let cool slightly,
then cut into ¼-inch-thick slices. Melt 5 tablespoons of the butter
in a large skillet and fry the potato slices until just golden. Cut the
apples into ¼-inch slices. Preheat the oven to 350°F. Line an 8-inch
square or round baking dish with parchment paper. Layer the potato,
apple, and Camembert slices in the dish, seasoning with sea salt and
pepper as you go and repeating the layers until all the ingredients
are used. Grease a piece of aluminum foil with the remaining
1 tablespoon butter and cover the baking dish, sealing it well. Place
in a roasting pan and fill with boiling water halfway up the sides
of the baking dish. Bake for 20 minutes. Cool for 10 minutes, then
turn out onto a serving platter. Remove the parchment paper.

*Optional: Decorate with thin slices of apple and serve hot as a
vegetarian main or as a side with roast pork or chicken.*

Citrus-Glazed Ham

You cannot stop the "oooohs" and "aaaahs" when
this lands center table on Christmas Day.

SERVES 8

One 10- to 12-pound bone-in, cured and smoked ham
1 cup orange marmalade
½ cup packed light brown sugar
4 oranges, cut into thin rounds

Put an oven shelf in the lowest position and preheat the oven to
350°F. If the rind is still on the ham, peel it away using a sharp knife;
you want just a thin layer of fat on the surface. Transfer the ham
to a large roasting pan or large rimmed baking sheet. In a small
saucepan over low heat, cook and stir the marmalade and sugar until
combined. Brush all over to glaze the ham. Arrange the orange slices,
overlapping, on top. Secure the slices with toothpicks if needed.
Brush with a little more glaze. Bake for 1 hour and 20 minutes,
brushing occasionally with the remaining glaze. Serve hot or cold.

Tip: To remove the rind, use a small sharp knife to cut through it. Cut along the
shank and, using your thumb, separate the edges of the meat from the fat.

Feta-Stuffed Chicken Breasts

This is a go-to dinner party main for me any time of the year.
Try these other stuffing ideas: Brie and caramelized onions;
ham and Swiss cheese; Parmesan, prosciutto, and basil.

SERVES 8

8 skinless, boneless chicken breast halves (6 to 6½ ounces each)
20 oil-packed sun-dried tomatoes, drained and chopped
7 ounces feta, crumbled
¼ cup coarsely chopped fresh tarragon

Preheat the oven to 350°F. Line a baking sheet with parchment
paper. Using a long, thin knife, cut a pocket into the thick part
of each breast, being careful not to cut through. Mix together
the tomatoes, feta, and tarragon. Fill the pockets with the
tomato mixture and secure the opening with a toothpick. Rub
the breasts with the oil from the tomatoes, season with sea salt
and pepper, and place on the baking sheet. Bake for 30 to 35
minutes, basting occasionally, until cooked through. Let rest for
5 minutes before serving to the pleasure of your guests.

*Optional: For goodness and color I simply serve this main
with steamed broccolini and roasted cherry tomatoes.*

Guard of Honor

The loveliness of lamb. What more can I say?

SERVES 8

Lamb racks totaling 24 chops
1 tablespoon olive oil
¼ cup dukkah (see Tip)
¼ cup chopped pistachios

Preheat the oven to 350°F. Trim excess fat from the lamb and wrap aluminum foil "crowns" around each bone to prevent burning. Drizzle the olive oil over the lamb and season with sea salt and pepper. Heat a large skillet and sear the lamb, in batches if necessary. Transfer to a baking sheet, bone side down. Mix the dukkah and pistachios and use to coat the meat, pressing firmly. Bake for 40 minutes for medium (or 25 minutes per pound), or until cooked to your preferred doneness. Remove the "crowns" before standing the racks on a platter, bones up and interleaved. Cut into chops to serve.

Tip: Dukkah originated in Egypt. It is a blend of roasted hazelnuts, sesame seeds, salt, pepper, and ground spices such as coriander, cumin, cinnamon, and turmeric. You can buy it online or experiment and make your own blend.

Maple & Pepper–Glazed Turkey

I tried several glazes but came to the realization that
the simplest was the best. How wonderful!

SERVES 8

One 12-pound turkey
4 tablespoons (½ stick) butter, melted
½ cup maple syrup
½ cup fresh sage leaves

Preheat the oven to 400°F. Place the turkey in a roasting pan, breast up, and tie the legs together with kitchen twine. Stir together 3 tablespoons of the butter and all of the syrup and brush over the entire turkey. Season generously all over with cracked pepper. Cover the bird loosely with aluminum foil. Roast for 30 minutes, then reduce the heat to 325°F. Continue to roast for another 3 hours, basting every 30 minutes and removing the foil for the last 30 minutes. Remove the turkey from the oven and transfer to a large serving platter. Cover loosely with foil and let rest for 30 minutes before carving. Do *not* slice the turkey before those 30 minutes are up, or else all the juices will flow out of the bird! To serve, place the sage in a skillet with the remaining 1 tablespoon butter and gently fry until crisp. Serve scattered across the turkey.

Tip: An easy way to see if your turkey is cooked is to insert a skewer into the thickest part of the thigh. The juices should run clear.

Hint: This turkey graces my Christmas table with sides of roasted onions, Brussels sprouts, and carrots, and an extra touch of sausage wound with thin strips of bacon.

Roast Pork & Crispy Crackling

※

Check out the piece of crackling missing! On the day of the
photo shoot, my beautiful sister-in-law, Nelly, who was heavily
pregnant, thought the shot had already been taken . . .

SERVES 8

One 6-pound pork shoulder, rind on
3 tablespoons olive oil
Juice of 1 lemon

Preheat the oven to 425°F. Place the pork in a roasting pan, rind side up.
Using a sharp knife, score the rind at ½-inch intervals, cutting deeply
almost into the fat layer. Rub 2 tablespoons of the olive oil into the rind
and drizzle with the lemon juice. Generously sprinkle 2 tablespoons sea
salt flakes over the rind and press into the scores. Drizzle the remaining
1 tablespoon oil in the pan and roast for 20 minutes. Reduce the heat to
350°F and cook for another 2 hours (or about 30 minutes per pound).

*Optional: For great crackling, look for a good coverage of fat and rind.
You might have to special-order from your butcher to get the rind.*

Rosemary & Chicken Arrows

MAKES 16 SKEWERS

16 long sprigs rosemary
4 skinless, boneless chicken breast halves
2 tablespoons honey
Finely shredded zest and juice of 1 lemon

Pick most of the leaves from the rosemary sprigs, leaving a few at one end. Soak the stems in cold water. Gently pound each breast to flatten it slightly. Cut each into four strips and place in a bowl. Chop the rosemary leaves and add to the chicken along with the honey, lemon zest, and juice, and season with sea salt and pepper. Mix to coat the chicken well. Cover and chill for at least 1 hour. Heat a grill, grill pan, or broiler to medium-high heat. Thread a strip of chicken onto each rosemary arrow. Cook the skewers for 5 to 6 minutes, turning occasionally, until cooked through.

Optional: Substitute strips of boneless lamb loin or chunks of vegetables, such as zucchini, onions, mushrooms, and red peppers (slip in some pineapple for sweetness) for the chicken. Garnishing with small rosemary sprigs is not only a pretty way to present, but a very tasty way, too.

Salmon Terrine

Use this as a sophisticated starter or main for any occasion.
Sometimes I will also add a handful of capers to the
cream cheese and lemon, which complement well.

SERVES 8 OR 12 AS A STARTER

1 pound sliced smoked salmon
1 envelope (¼ ounce) unflavored gelatin
Two 8-ounce packages chive and onion cream cheese, softened
Finely shredded zest and juice of ½ lemon

Line a 9-inch loaf pan with parchment paper overhanging the sides.
Line the pan with smoked salmon, laying slices lengthwise across the
base and up the four sides, leaving enough overlap to fold over the
top of the filling. Set aside enough smoked salmon to make a middle
layer the length of the pan, then chop the remaining salmon into small
pieces. Mix the gelatin with 3 tablespoons hot water until dissolved.
Beat the cream cheese, chopped salmon, lemon juice, and gelatin
until well combined. Spoon half the cheese filling into the pan. Lay the
reserved smoked salmon slices on top, then spoon on the rest of the
filling and smooth the top. Tap the pan on the work surface to expel
any trapped air. Fold the overhanging salmon to cover the top. Cover
with plastic wrap and chill for at least 4 hours or overnight. To serve,
unwrap, carefully turn the loaf out of the pan onto a serving platter,
remove the parchment, sprinkle with the lemon zest, and slice.

Sweet Squash Galette

Possibly one of my all-time favorite vegetarian meals.

SERVES 8

2 pounds winter squash (such as acorn or butternut),
peeled, seeded, and cut into 2-inch wedges
2 sheets puff pastry, thawed if frozen, cut in half lengthwise
1 cup sour cream
1 cup sweet chili sauce

Preheat the oven to 400°F. Lightly grease one baking sheet and line
another two with parchment paper. Place the squash wedges on the
greased baking sheet and bake for 15 to 20 minutes. Remove from
the oven and let cool slightly. Join together the two halves of one
pastry sheet to create a long rectangular strip and roll in 1 inch of
the dough to create a lip around the edge. Repeat with the second
pastry sheet. Place each dough length on a parchment paper–lined
baking sheet. Spread half the sour cream over each base. Lay the
roasted squash on top, season with cracked pepper, and drizzle
generously with sweet chili sauce. Bake for 20 to 25 minutes, until
the pastry edges are puffed and golden. Serve hot or warm.

*Hint: Before baking, brush the pastry with beaten egg for a golden
finish. Garnish with fresh sage for a hint of added flavor.*

Wild Mushroom Beef Wellington

SERVES 8

3 pounds filet of beef in one piece
1 pound mushrooms, sliced
2 sheets puff pastry, thawed if frozen
8 ounces peppercorn pâté

Preheat the oven to 350°F. Remove all fat from the meat. Tie the beef in four places with kitchen twine so it holds its cylindrical shape while cooking. Season with sea salt and cracked pepper. In a hot nonstick skillet, sear the meat all over, including the ends, about 4 minutes. Transfer the meat to a baking sheet and roast for 10 minutes. Remove from the oven and let cool completely. Raise the oven temperature to 475°F. Meanwhile, in the same skillet, cook the mushrooms for 6 minutes, or until most of the liquid has evaporated. Lightly season with sea salt and pepper and set aside to cool. As soon as both the meat and mushrooms are cool, join the two sheets of puff pastry together. Trim off a thin strip for decoration. Beat the pâté until soft and spread liberally over the pastry, leaving a 1½-inch border. Top with the mushrooms. Remove the twine from the cooled filet and place the meat on top of the mushrooms. Wrap like a present, making sure the filet is totally encased. Line a baking sheet with parchment paper and transfer the wrapped filet to the baking sheet, seam side down. Decorate the top with thin strips of pastry and cracked black pepper. Bake for 5 minutes, then lower the temperature to 350°F and bake for 45 minutes for medium doneness. Let rest for 10 minutes before transferring to a platter, slicing, and serving.

*Hint: Before baking, brush the pastry with beaten
egg for a gorgeous golden finish.*

Sides

A Plate of Asparagus

SERVES 8

2 pounds asparagus, woody ends snapped off

Heat a grill, grill pan, or cast-iron skillet to medium. Spray
lightly with nonstick cooking spray. Cook the asparagus
for 4 minutes, in batches if necessary, turning regularly,
until tender. Serve with the accompanying sauces.

PARMESAN BUTTER

2 tablespoons butter, melted

¼ cup thinly shaved
Parmesan cheese

Combine the butter and
Parmesan in a small bowl.
Dollop over the asparagus
and sprinkle with sea salt
and cracked pepper.

BALSAMIC SALSA

2 tablespoons olive oil

1 tablespoon balsamic vinegar

1 tomato, peeled, seeded,
and finely chopped

1 tablespoon finely
chopped basil leaves

Combine all the ingredients in
a small bowl and gently season
with sea salt and pepper. Drizzle
over the asparagus spears.

TOASTED PINE NUTS

1 tablespoon butter

3 tablespoons pine nuts

1 teaspoon fresh lemon juice

In a small nonstick skillet
over medium heat, combine
the ingredients and cook,
stirring regularly, for 2 to 3
minutes, until the pine nuts
are browned. Serve scattered
over the asparagus spears.

Golden Roast Potatoes

SERVES 8

3½ pounds Yukon Gold, red-skinned, or fingerling potatoes
¼ cup olive oil
16 cloves garlic, unpeeled
Finely shredded zest of 1 lemon

Wash the potatoes and pop them into a saucepan large enough to hold them in a single layer. Add salt and enough water to just cover. Bring to a boil. Cover and reduce the heat. Simmer for 10 to 20 minutes, or until tender when tested with a skewer. Drain and return to the saucepan. Place over medium heat for 2 minutes to dry the potatoes. While the potatoes are cooking, preheat the oven to 400°F. Pour the oil into a roasting pan and place in the oven for 2 minutes, or until really hot. Squash the potatoes gently with a potato masher so that the skins burst. Remove the roasting pan from the oven and add the potatoes and garlic cloves. Toss to coat completely in the oil. Roast for 45 minutes, or until crispy, flipping them after 20 to 25 minutes. Remove the potatoes and garlic from the pan, drain off the excess oil, pop the garlic from its skin, season with sea salt and pepper, and serve sprinkled with lemon zest.

Green Beans with Garlic & Lemony Butter

SERVES 8

3 tablespoons butter, softened
Finely shredded zest of 1 lemon
1 clove garlic, finely chopped
1 pound green beans, trimmed

Put the butter, zest, and garlic in a medium bowl and stir until well combined. Season with salt and pepper, cover, and chill in the refrigerator. Meanwhile, bring a large saucepan of water to a boil, add a pinch of salt, and cook the beans for 2 to 3 minutes, until just tender. Drain and transfer to a serving dish. Dollop with the butter mixture. Toss and serve.

Optional: For presentation, wrap equal amounts of beans with a cucumber ribbon.

Honey-Glazed Sweet Potatoes

While I was backpacking around England in the early 1990s, my Kiwi friends introduced me to the delights of baked sweet potatoes ("kumara" to them). This recipe is so good, it now graces my Christmas table annually.

SERVES 8

5½ pounds sweet potatoes

¾ cup honey

2 tablespoons lightly chopped rosemary leaves

Preheat the oven to 400°F. Line a baking sheet with parchment paper. Peel the sweet potatoes and cut them into 1-inch-wide slices. Combine the honey and rosemary in a large bowl, add the sweet potatoes, season with sea salt and pepper, and toss to coat. Place on the baking sheet and roast for 20 to 25 minutes, or until tender and caramelized.

Sauce & Gravy

I love my meat with rich, flavorful sauces and gravy. I'm constantly surprised at how many people struggle with them. Here are two that are among my favorites.

SERVES 8

CREAMY PEPPERCORN SAUCE

2 tablespoons canned green peppercorns, rinsed and drained
1 cup heavy cream
2/3 cup dry white wine

Combine all the ingredients in a small saucepan and gently bring to a boil, stirring regularly. Season with sea salt and pepper, reduce the heat, and simmer for 10 minutes, or until slightly thickened.

Optional: If serving this with roast beef, add the pan juices to flavor the sauce.

GLORIOUS GRAVY

1/4 cup pan drippings, excess fat skimmed off
1 tablespoon all-purpose flour
1 cup stock

Place the roasting pan with drippings over a low flame. Using a wire whisk, stir in the flour until a light brown paste forms. Gradually pour in the stock, whisking all the time, until you have a thickened gravy. Season with sea salt and cracked pepper and simmer for 2 minutes, scraping any sticky bits from the sides of the pan (they contribute to a richly flavored gravy).

Seasoned Roast Vegetables

I *love* this dish. I serve it at least once a week year-round, using whatever veggies are in season. My favorite roasted vegetable is beets—divine!

SERVES 8

8 slender carrots, peeled
4 large parsnips, peeled, cut in half or quarters, and cored
2 beets, peeled and cut into thick wedges
½ cup olive oil

Preheat the oven to 400°F. Place the vegetables in a large baking dish. Season well with sea salt and cracked pepper, drizzle generously with the olive oil, and toss them to coat evenly. Bake, stirring the vegetables occasionally, for 45 minutes, or until tender and golden brown. Transfer to a platter to accompany a roasted main course.

Desserts

Caramel Ice Cream

When I made this on a national morning show in Australia, the switchboard jammed with inbound calls. If you have to travel to buy dulce de leche, do so. Your guests will praise your efforts for weeks!

SERVES 8

1¼ cups heavy cream, chilled
One 13.4-ounce can dulce de leche

Line a 9-inch loaf pan with parchment paper. In a large bowl, beat the cream until soft peaks form. Fold in the dulce de leche until combined. Transfer to the pan, cover with plastic wrap, and freeze overnight. To serve, allow to soften briefly in the fridge, then scoop out into serving dishes.

Optional: Serve with additional dulce de leche drizzled over the top or garnished with fresh sweet raspberries and toasted coconut.

Hint: To make your own delectable dulce de leche, remove the label from a 14-ounce can of sweetened condensed milk and place the unopened can in a saucepan. Cover with water by at least 1 inch and bring to a boil. Simmer for 1½ to 2 hours for runny dulce de leche, or up to 4 hours for a more solid consistency. Add more boiling water to the pan when required to keep the can covered.

Chocolate Tofu Mousse

SERVES 4

12 ounces silken tofu, drained, at room temperature
8 ounces dark chocolate, chopped
2 tablespoons pure maple syrup
1 teaspoon vanilla extract

Puree the tofu in a blender (or with a stick blender) until just smooth. In a medium microwave-safe bowl, melt the chocolate, stirring every 30 seconds, until nice and smooth. Add the maple syrup and vanilla and stir to combine. Add the tofu and mix until creamy. Spoon the mixture into four small serving dishes or tall champagne flutes. Chill for 2 hours, or until set.

Optional: When entertaining, I garnish this with long shards of chocolate and a dollop of whipped cream for an impressive finish.

Christmas Fruitcake

I have included this recipe in the American edition because with these three simple ingredients you will make one of the most popular cakes in British and Australian history: a fruitcake! This one in particular is special, as it has no added sugar in it.

SERVES 10

2¼ pounds mixed chopped dried fruit
3 cups fruit juice (I use whatever is on sale: apple, orange, cranberry, and so on)
3 cups self-rising flour

Soak the dried fruit in the juice overnight. Preheat the oven to 250°F. Line a 9-inch round cake pan with parchment paper. Stir the flour into the soaked fruit and mix well. Spoon the batter into the pan. Bake on the lowest rack in the oven for 2½ hours, or until a skewer inserted in the center comes out clean. Remove from the oven and let cool in the pan on a wire rack. Turn the cake out onto a serving platter and peel off the parchment paper. To keep, wrap the cake in aluminum foil or place in an airtight container. This cake will keep nicely for up to 4 weeks if not devoured prior.

Optional: Add a shot of your favorite tipple—brandy, rum, sherry, or Grand Marnier—to the fruit when soaking.

Hint: Decorate as you wish with cherries, nuts, candied ginger, or as I have done—with a rich chocolate ganache made by heating 1 cup heavy cream and stirring in 8 ounces chopped dark chocolate until nice and thick. Refrigerate until cooled to spreading temperature.

Custards

From babies to grandparents, we love our thick, creamy custards—
and Christmas just wouldn't be the same without them to
accompany Christmas fruitcake, plum pudding, and trifle!

BRANDY CUSTARD

SERVES 4

2 cups milk
6 egg yolks
½ cup superfine sugar
1 tablespoon brandy

Place the milk in a large saucepan and bring
to a simmer over medium-high heat. Remove
from the heat and set aside to cool slightly.
Whisk together the egg yolks and sugar in a
heatproof bowl. Gradually whisk in the warm
milk. Pour the custard back into the saucepan
and cook over low heat, stirring constantly,
for 10 minutes, or until the custard coats
the back of the spoon. Add the brandy and
stir to combine. Serve warm or chilled.

*Optional: Add ½ teaspoon vanilla extract
to the eggs, if in your pantry.*

*Hint: Now that you have all of those egg whites left
over, try making the Garden Bed Pavlova on page 116!*

CREAMY CUSTARD

SERVES 4

½ cup sugar
4 egg yolks
1¼ cups heavy cream, whipped to soft peaks

Combine the sugar and 1 cup water in a small
saucepan. Stir over medium heat, without
allowing to boil, until the sugar dissolves. Bring to
a boil. Simmer uncovered, without stirring, until
the syrup is reduced to about ½ cup. Beat the egg
yolks in a heatproof bowl with an electric mixer
until thick and creamy. Gradually pour in the
hot syrup in a thin stream, beating continuously
until the mixture is thick and creamy. Fold in
the cream. Refrigerate until ready to serve.

Fruitcake–Ice Cream Terrine

This was my favorite dessert last Christmas. Simply stunning!

SERVES 8

1 pound fruitcake (homemade, page 110, or store-bought), cut into 1-inch slices
3 tablespoons Cointreau
1 tablespoon finely grated orange zest
1½ quarts vanilla ice cream, softened

Line a 9-inch loaf pan with plastic wrap. Brush the cake slices
with the Cointreau. Stir the orange zest into the ice cream.
Spread half the ice cream mixture in the pan. Top with the cake
slices, then the remaining ice cream. Cover completely with
plastic wrap and freeze overnight. When ready to serve, unwrap,
carefully turn the terrine out onto a serving platter, and peel off
the plastic. Use a hot knife to cut into eight delicious slices.

Garden Bed Pavlova

This was inspired by the food halls of Harrods in London, Christmas 2009. Topped with edible flowers, it transforms a classic Aussie dessert into art. It's almost too pretty to eat!

SERVES 8

5 egg whites
1¼ cups superfine sugar
1 tablespoon cornstarch
Edible flowers, such as petunias and nasturtiums

Preheat the oven to 275°F. Line a large baking sheet with parchment paper. Beat the egg whites in a large bowl with an electric mixer until soft peaks form. Gradually add the sugar, beating until it dissolves, scraping down the side of the bowl occasionally, until stiff peaks form. Use a rubber spatula to fold in the cornstarch. Pile the meringue in the center of the baking sheet, then with the spatula, spread the meringue in a 9-inch circle, making a shallow well in the center. Put the pan in the lower half of the oven and immediately lower the temperature to 225°F. Bake for 1½ hours, or until dry and crisp. Turn off the oven and let the pavlova cool in the oven with the door ajar. Serve topped with whipped cream and randomly scattered edible flowers.

Hint: Not all flowers are edible, but here are some that are: lavender, thyme, dill, cilantro, day lily, zucchini flowers, nasturtiums, petunias, chives, and basil. Just make sure they haven't been sprayed with insecticide. In addition, I candied some of our neighbor's rose petals by brushing them with egg whites and dusting with superfine sugar. I did this a day ahead of time to allow time for setting.

Mincemeat Meringue Tarts

MAKES 24 TARTS

2 sheets refrigerated pie crust pastry
One 27-ounce jar mincemeat
1 cup sugar
2 egg whites

Preheat the oven to 350°F. Roll the pastry out onto a clean, flat surface. Using a 3-inch cookie cutter with a scalloped edge, cut 24 rounds (patch and recut if necessary). Gently press the rounds into two 12-cup muffin pans. Bake for 5 minutes. Remove from the oven and fill each pastry cup with about 1½ tablespoons mincemeat. Stir together the sugar and ¼ cup water in a small saucepan until the sugar dissolves, then bring to a boil. Cook undisturbed until the syrup reaches about 235°F or soft-ball stage (a teaspoonful will form a soft ball when dropped into cold water). While the syrup is cooking, start beating the egg whites with a mixer to medium peaks. Pour the syrup down the side of the bowl in a slow, steady stream, taking care not to pour it on the beaters. Continue beating until thick and glossy. Pipe or spoon the meringue over the tarts. Return to the oven and bake for 5 minutes, or until golden. Serve warm or at room temperature.

Optional: Cut star shapes from any remaining pastry and place them on some of the tarts instead of the meringue. Brush with beaten egg and sprinkle with Demerara sugar. Bake at 350°F for 15 to 20 minutes.

Plum Pudding

Christmas just wouldn't be the same without boiled plum pudding;
it's a tradition. Here is the simplest recipe for it I've ever made.

SERVES 12

2 cups self-rising flour

1 cup superfine sugar

2 pounds mixed dried fruit

1 tablespoon baking soda

Mix the flour, sugar, and fruit in a large bowl. In a separate bowl, mix
2 cups boiling water with the baking soda. Add to the flour–fruit mixture
and stir or fold well. Cover and leave overnight. Mix well the next
morning. Dampen a clean cotton kitchen towel and sprinkle it lightly
with flour. Turn the pudding out of the bowl onto the towel and gather
the towel together to form the pudding into a ball. Tie very securely
with kitchen twine. Place the wrapped pudding in a large saucepan and
fill with water until just covered. Bring to a boil, then reduce the heat
and simmer for 3 hours, making sure the pudding is always well covered
with water. Cool slightly before carefully peeling off the towel so as not
to disrupt the delicious, thick skin that forms. Slice in wedges to serve.

*Optional: Serve with a drizzle of cream or scoop of ice cream or, as
my family does, with Creamy Custard (page 112), garnished with
chocolate-dipped fruit, twigs of holly, or a Christmas decoration.*

Roly-Poly Trifle

In Australia and New Zealand, every nana, mum, and aunt has her own "secret" trifle recipe. This is mine, and now it's yours, too. Enjoy!

SERVES 8

One 17-ounce jelly roll (store-bought or homemade)
2 cups heavy cream
1 envelope (¼ ounce) unflavored gelatin
2 pints strawberries

Line a deep round bowl (so that when turned upside down, it is a dome shape) with plastic wrap. Slice the jelly roll into ½-inch-thick slices and line the entire bowl with them. Whip the cream until stiff peaks form. Mix the gelatin with 3 tablespoons warm water, stirring vigorously until dissolved, then beat into the cream. Chop 1½ pints of the strawberries and stir into the cream. Pour the strawberry–cream mixture over the cake slices in the bowl and smooth the top. Cover with plastic wrap and chill in the fridge for 3 to 4 hours, until set. When ready to serve, unwrap, carefully turn out onto a serving platter, remove the bowl, and peel off the plastic. Decorate with the remaining strawberries and serve.

Rum & Raisin Decadence

This is the reason I love ice cream.

SERVES 8

1 cup raisins

½ cup dark rum

1½ quarts chocolate chip ice cream, softened

8 ounces chocolate-coated macadamia nuts (about ¾ of an 11-ounce bag), cut in half

Line a 9-inch loaf pan with parchment paper. Soak the raisins
in the rum for 2 to 3 hours. In a large bowl, whip the ice cream
until peaks are just starting to form. Fold in the raisin mixture and
two-thirds of the macadamia nuts. Scrape the mixture into the
pan. Cover with plastic wrap and freeze overnight. When ready
to serve, unwrap, turn out onto a chilled serving platter, peel
off the parchment paper, and top with the remaining nuts.

White Christmas Cheesecake

SERVES 8

8 ounces cream cheese, softened
One 14-ounce can sweetened condensed milk
1 envelope (¼ ounce) unflavored gelatin
5 ounces white chocolate, chopped

In a medium bowl, beat the cream cheese until smooth. Add the condensed milk and continue beating until well combined. Dissolve the gelatin in 3 tablespoons warm water, stirring vigorously. Add to the cheese mixture. Pour into your favorite crust (see options below) and chill for at least 4 hours. Line a baking sheet with parchment paper. About 30 minutes before serving, melt the chocolate in a clean, dry microwave-safe bowl, stirring every 30 seconds until nice and smooth. Pour the chocolate onto the baking sheet and spread it out evenly. Refrigerate for 15 minutes. Remove and with a sharp knife, cut long, thin shards from the chocolate, enough to completely cover the top of the cheesecake.

Optional: There are a number of really easy recipes available for baked pastry, graham cracker, or cookie crumb crusts. Or you can always purchase prepared versions. Choose whichever you prefer for this fabulous filling.

Sweet Treats

A Box of Chocolates

Thank you, Nabisco, for giving the world the most versatile cookie ever!

MAKES ABOUT 30 PIECES

⅔ package (15.5 ounces) Oreo cookies (about 25 cookies)
4 ounces cream cheese, softened
5 to 6 ounces milk chocolate, chopped

Line a baking sheet with parchment paper. In a food processor, grind the cookies to a fine meal. Add the cream cheese and blend until well combined with no traces of white. Use a teaspoon to scoop out portions of the mixture. Roll into balls, place on the baking sheet, and refrigerate for 30 minutes. In a medium microwave-safe bowl, melt the chocolate, stirring every 30 seconds, until nice and smooth. Using a fork or two teaspoons, dip the chilled balls one at a time and coat thoroughly; drain excess chocolate. Place back on the tray. When all are coated, refrigerate to set.

Optional: When ready to serve, remove the truffles from the fridge and let sit out for 10 minutes so they begin to sweat. This makes it easier for coatings to stick. Here are the options we used:

Shredded coconut • Crushed nuts • Crushed pistachios • Cocoa powder • Melted white chocolate • Edible glitter • Decorating sugar crystals • Sea salt flakes

Angel Wings

MAKES 24 PIECES

7 ounces white chocolate, chopped
24 plump dried apricots
½ cup unsalted shelled pistachios, finely chopped

Line a baking sheet with parchment paper. In a microwave-safe bowl, melt the chocolate, stirring every 30 seconds, until nice and smooth. One at a time, dip the apricots in the melted chocolate, covering only half, then dip the chocolate end in the pistachios. Place on the baking sheet. Refrigerate for 10 minutes, or until set. Pop into an airtight jar or container and keep refrigerated until ready to serve.

Cherry Baubles

At my Christmas street party last year, I served a tray of these. A gentlemanly neighbor picked one up and in utter amazement asked, "How did you make these?" He had no idea why all the women started laughing!

MAKES 24 BAUBLES

5 to 6 ounces milk chocolate, chopped
24 plump ripe cherries with stems

In a medium microwave-safe bowl, melt the chocolate, stirring every 30 seconds, until nice and smooth. Line a baking sheet with parchment paper. Take one cherry at a time and dip it halfway in the melted chocolate, then place on the baking sheet. Repeat until all the cherries are covered. Chill until ready to serve.

Tip: Although cherries are out of season in the United States at Christmas, remember these for your next Fourth of July festivities. They are too lovely!

Choc-Cherry Fudge

B.R.I.L.L.I.A.N.T.

MAKES 16 PIECES

8 ounces dark chocolate, chopped
One 14-ounce can sweetened condensed milk
1 cup walnuts, chopped
16 maraschino cherries with stems

Line an 8-inch square baking pan with parchment paper, leaving an overhang on two sides. In a large microwave-safe bowl, melt the chocolate in the condensed milk on medium-high for 4 minutes, checking at regular intervals. Stir vigorously to combine. Stir in the nuts and spread in the pan. Lightly score the top with a knife to create squares, first in half, then quarters, eighths, and finally sixteenths. Gently press a pretty red cherry into the center of each square. Refrigerate to set. Remove the fudge from the pan by lifting it out with the paper overhang and place on a cutting board. Cut along the lines and serve.

Chocolate-Coated Orange Candy

These are my dad's all-time favorite sweets. I make them at
Christmas, on his July 10 birthday, and for Father's Day, which
we celebrate in September. And several times throughout
the year as payment for taking my boys fishing.

SERVES 8

4 oranges

1 cup sugar

8 ounces dark chocolate, chopped

Quarter and peel each orange. (Set aside the orange segments for
another use.) Cut the peel into ¼-inch strips, leaving the pith intact.
Place the strips in a saucepan of cold water and bring to a boil. Drain
and repeat the process once more. Meanwhile, in another saucepan,
combine the sugar with 1½ cups water and a pinch of salt. Cook
over medium heat until clear. Add the orange peel and simmer for
40 minutes, or until all the syrup is absorbed and the peel is transparent.
Using a slotted spoon, transfer the strips to wire racks for 3 hours, or until
dry. Line a baking sheet with parchment paper. In a medium microwave-
safe bowl, melt the chocolate, stirring every 30 seconds, until nice
and smooth. Dip each piece of orange candy in the chocolate three-
quarters of the length and place on the baking sheet. Refrigerate to set.

*Optional: Use the remainder of your oranges for fresh juice
or in the Ruby Jeweled Lobster Salad on page 66.*

Christmas Glitter Pops

Fruitcake and rum are the main ingredients in my rum balls.
With this recipe, I have just added a little glitz and glitter.

MAKES 24 POPS

1 pound fruitcake (homemade, page 110, or store-bought)
½ cup dark rum
12 ounces white chocolate, chopped
Edible glitter

Place the cake and rum in a food processor and process until combined. Refrigerate for 30 minutes. Line a baking sheet with parchment paper. Use a teaspoon to scoop out generous portions of the mixture. Roll into balls and place on the baking sheet. In a medium microwave-safe bowl, melt the chocolate, stirring every 20 seconds, until creamy. Roll each ball in chocolate and return to the baking sheet. Chill for 15 minutes, or until set. About 10 minutes before serving, remove from the fridge and let sit out to sweat. Roll each ball thoroughly in edible glitter and gently pierce with a lollipop stick before serving to the delight of all.

Cinnamon Stars

MAKES 24 COOKIES

2 egg whites
2¼ cups powdered sugar, sifted
1½ cups almond meal
1 tablespoon ground cinnamon

Beat the egg whites lightly with a wooden spoon in a large bowl. Gradually stir in the powdered sugar to form a smooth icing. Transfer ⅓ cup to a small bowl, cover tightly, and set aside. Add the almond meal and cinnamon to the remaining icing and gently press together with your hands. Add 1 teaspoon water if the dough seems too dry. Press together well before adding any water, as the warmth of your hands will soften the dough. Lightly dust a clean work surface with powdered sugar and roll out the dough to about ⅛ inch thick. Spread with a thin layer of the reserved icing. Leave uncovered at room temperature for 30 to 35 minutes, until the icing has set. Preheat the oven to 300°F. Line a baking sheet with parchment paper. Cut out shapes using a variety of star cookie cutters (dipping the cutters in powdered sugar to help prevent sticking). Place on the baking sheet and bake for 10 minutes, or until just firm. Let cool on the sheet. Store in an airtight container until ready to serve.

Coconut Truffles

MAKES 24 TRUFFLES

⅓ cup thick coconut milk
1 cup unsweetened shredded coconut
8 ounces white chocolate, chopped
1 tablespoon butter

In a medium saucepan, bring the coconut milk and ¾ cup of the shredded coconut to a simmer. Remove from the heat and stir in the chocolate. Let sit for about 5 minutes to melt. Add the butter and stir to combine. Cover and chill for 3 hours. Line a baking sheet with parchment paper. Use a teaspoon to scoop out a portion of the mixture. Roll into a ball, then roll in the remaining coconut until coated. Place on the baking sheet. Repeat until the mixture runs out. Chill for at least 2 hours before serving.

Hint: These make a thoughtful gift packaged in a clear box or in a cellophane bag tied with pretty ribbon for any occasion.

Lime & Macadamia Fudge

MAKES 24 PIECES

One 14-ounce can sweetened condensed milk
18 ounces white chocolate, chopped
1¼ cups chopped macadamia nuts
Finely grated zest of 2 limes

Line an 8-inch square baking pan with parchment paper. Place the condensed milk and chocolate in a saucepan and stir over low heat until smooth. Remove from the heat. Add the nuts and zest and mix well. Pour into the pan and refrigerate overnight prior to cutting.

Marzipan Marbles

MAKES 40 PIECES

2½ rolls (7 ounces each) almond paste, broken into pieces
4½ cups powdered sugar
½ cup light corn syrup
40 pecan halves

Place the almond paste and powdered sugar in an electric mixer with a paddle and beat until combined. Add the corn syrup and continue to beat until well combined. (If your mixer can't hold that much, work with half of each ingredient at a time.) Turn out onto a clean work surface and knead the marzipan until a smooth dough forms. Line a baking sheet with parchment paper. Use a tablespoon to scoop out portions of the marzipan. Roll into balls and pop onto the baking sheet. Firmly press a pecan into the center of each ball. Set aside for 4 hours, or until firm.

Peppermint Crème Checkers

MAKES 24 PIECES

8 ounces dark chocolate, chopped
8 ounces white chocolate, chopped
20 Oreo Cool Mint Crème cookies
4 ounces cream cheese, softened

In a medium microwave-safe bowl, melt the dark chocolate, stirring every 30 seconds, until silky smooth. In a chocolate mold with 12 square cavities (or an ice cube tray) spoon enough chocolate to coat just the base. In a separate bowl, melt the white chocolate. Coat the base of another 12-cavity mold. Refrigerate the molds to set. Meanwhile, grind the cookies in a food processor to a fine meal. Add the cream cheese and blend until well combined. Remove the chocolate molds from the fridge. Use a teaspoon to scoop out a portion of the mixture, roll into a ball, and pop it onto a chocolate base. Lightly press to spread almost to the edges. Repeat until all the cavities are filled. Remelt the chocolates, if necessary, and spoon in, covering the filling. Refrigerate for 30 minutes, or until set.

Optional: If you don't have chocolate molds or don't want to use ice cube trays, it's just as easy to roll the cookie mixture into balls and dip them in melted chocolate to coat.

Reindeer Bark

I have made this for my children's teachers as a
Christmas gift for the last three years.

SERVES 8

4 peppermint candy canes
7 ounces dark chocolate, chopped

Seal the candy canes in a heavy-duty plastic bag, squeezing out all
the air. Wrap the bag in a kitchen towel, place on a hard surface, and
pound with a rolling pin until the canes are crushed. In a microwave-
safe bowl, melt the chocolate, stirring every 30 seconds, until silky
smooth. Line a baking sheet with parchment paper. Pour the chocolate
onto the baking sheet and spread it to about ⅛ inch thick. Sprinkle
with the crushed candy. Set aside for 20 minutes to set, or in the fridge
if room temperature is too warm. Break into pieces to serve. Store
the bark in an airtight container in a cool place for up to 5 days.

*Optional: Get creative! Another pretty gift idea is to substitute white
chocolate for the dark chocolate and scatter dried cranberries,
raisins, or pistachios on top instead of candy canes.*

Rocky Road Bonbons

I wrap these individually for birthday gifts, Valentine's Day, Christmas, or whenever I just want to say "thank you" throughout the year.

MAKES 16 PIECES

8 ounces dark, milk, or white chocolate, chopped
1 cup macadamia nuts, halved
1 cup marshmallows
5 ounces Turkish delight, coarsely chopped

In a medium microwave-safe bowl, melt the chocolate, stirring every 20 or 30 seconds, until nice and smooth. Allow to cool slightly before adding the nuts, marshmallows, and Turkish delight. Mix until well combined. Line an 8-inch square baking pan with parchment paper. Pour the mixture into it, neaten the edges, and refrigerate until set. Turn the candy out onto a cool cutting board and peel off the parchment paper. Cut into 16 squares. Wrap each in clear cellophane. These make a beautiful handmade Christmas gift tied at each end with a pretty ribbon.

Salted Caramel Charms

The combination of smooth, sweet caramel, crunchy salt crystals, and bittersweet chocolate may sound unusual, but it makes these little balls of loveliness impossible to stop at one.

MAKES 24 PIECES

⅓ cup sugar

⅔ cup heavy cream

8 ounces dark chocolate, chopped coarsely

7 ounces milk chocolate, chopped

Line a baking sheet with parchment paper. Mix the sugar with 2 tablespoons water in a medium saucepan over medium heat and stir until it dissolves. Bring to a gentle boil and let cook undisturbed until golden brown. Add the cream (it will bubble up!). Stir over low heat with a wooden spoon until the congealed toffee pieces melt and the mixture is smooth again. Remove from the heat and stir in the dark chocolate and ½ teaspoon sea salt flakes until the chocolate is melted. Set aside to cool and thicken. Line a baking sheet with parchment paper. Use a teaspoon to scoop out portions of the mixture. Roll into balls, place on the baking sheet, and freeze for 30 minutes. With 5 minutes to go, in a medium microwave-safe bowl, melt the milk chocolate, stirring every 20 seconds, until nice and smooth. Using two spoons, dip the candies in the milk chocolate to coat. Return to the baking sheet. Top each truffle with a small pinch of coarse sea salt. Refrigerate to set.

Drinks

Christmas Candy Martini

My absolute favorite Christmas cocktail.

SERVES 1

2 ounces vanilla-flavored vodka
1 ounce white chocolate liqueur
1 ounce peppermint schnapps
1 teaspoon grenadine

Fill a cocktail shaker with crushed ice. Add the vodka, liqueur,
and schnapps. Shake well and strain into a chilled cocktail glass.
Pour the grenadine slowly down the inside edge of the glass—
it will sink to the bottom, forming a gloriously colored base.

Festive Fruit Fizz

SERVES 8

1 cup cubed seeded watermelon
10 strawberries, hulled and halved
1 cup cubed fresh pineapple
1 liter lemon-lime soda or seltzer, well chilled

Spread the watermelon, strawberries, and pineapple on a baking sheet and place in the freezer for several hours, until frozen. Process the frozen fruit in a blender until smooth, in batches if necessary. Transfer the fruit puree to a large pitcher, add the soda, and stir. Serve over ice.

Tipsy Tip: *Add a little vodka for the adults.*

Mango Daiquiri

SERVES 4

1 mango, peeled, pitted, and chopped
Juice and very thinly sliced peel of 1 lime
1 tablespoon superfine sugar
6 ounces light rum, such as Bacardi

Place all the ingredients with 3 cups crushed ice in a blender and blend until smooth. Pour into chilled glasses and garnish with some of the lime peel.

Optional: For a thicker consistency, use frozen mango.

Mint Tea

Directly inspired by English tea houses during my stay there in winter 2010. A freshly brewed pot of mint tea cost an average of £5! I flew home and planted mint (delighting in the fact you can't kill it) and now enjoy it for free!

SERVES 4

20 fresh mint leaves, plus more for garnish
1 quart boiling water

Place the leaves in a tea pot. Pour in the water and steep for 3 to 4 minutes. Pour into individual cups garnished with 1 or 2 fresh mint leaves. Enjoy!

Watermelon Bellini

When I asked the waiter at Claridge's in London if they serve this drink by the pitcher he almost choked. I guess that was a negative?!?!

SERVES 8

1 lime
3 cups cubed seeded watermelon, chilled
1 cup unfiltered apple juice
One 750 ml bottle prosecco, chilled

Squeeze the lime and cut the rind into thin curls. Place the watermelon, 2 tablespoons of the lime juice, and the apple juice in a blender and process until smooth. Pour about ½ cup of the puree into each of eight champagne flutes and top with prosecco. Garnish with a curl of lime rind. Serve immediately.

Acknowledgments

As with all projects, mine only see the light of day because of the help
and contribution of others. These are my fabulous "others."

Janelle McCosker: My assistant researcher and stylist who secretly harbors a desire to leave it all behind and start a career rapping "Nelly on ze Block!" Watch out, J.Lo!

Melanie Roberts: What this lady can do with chocolate and candy is extraordinary.

Melinda Dines: Who in her motherly way ensured we were all fed and hydrated and who gathered props from Noosa to Neighbor.

Michelle Evans: Our link to the world. Life is simply "funner" with this lady in it. Is she Greek, Mexican, Italian, Kiwi? Who cares, she's lovely!

Katie Guiver: The most eager taste tester among us, what a dream you are.

Leonie Wohlsen: A calming influence in any situation. Can we have more of what she's having?

Jennette McCosker: "Grandma, you are a fabulous ingredient at any gathering. You add light and laughter. Don't ever change!"

Megan Slade: The Lady with the Lens. Megs, no wonder you have been my photographer of choice for three years.

Glen Turnbull: Who—had we registered—could possibly own the record for most trips to a supermarket in a day. You are a superstar husband!

You made such an almighty task, in such a short time, fun and exciting to be a part of.

With much love and gratitude,

Kim

Index

Invitation

JOIN OUR FOODIE FAMILY

At 4 Ingredients, we cultivate a family of busy people all bound together by the desire to create good, healthy, homemade meals quickly, easily, and economically. Our aim is to save us all precious time and money in the kitchen. If this is you, too, then we invite you to join our growing family where we share kitchen wisdom daily. If you have a favorite recipe, or a tip that has worked for you in your kitchen that you think others would enjoy it, please contact us at:

 facebook.com/4ingredientspage

 4 Ingredients

 4 Ingredients Channel

 4ingredients.com.au

@4ingredients

Happy Entertaining!

Kim